D1101427

dabblelab

ENGINEERING

PROJECTS TO BUILD ON

BY TAMMY ENZ

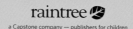

raintree

a Capstone company — publishers for children

Raintree is an imprint of Capstone Global Library Limited, a company incorporated in England and Wales
having its registered office at 264 Banbury Road, Oxford, OX2 7DY – Registered company number: 6695582

www.raintree.co.uk
myorders@raintree.co.uk

Text © Capstone Global Library Limited 2019
The moral rights of the proprietor have been asserted.

Edited by Mari Bolte
Designed by Heidi Thompson
Original illustrations © Capstone Global Library Limited 2019
Picture research by Morgan Walters
Production by Laura Manthe
Originated by Capstone Global Library Ltd
Printed and bound in India

ISBN 978 1 4747 7543 4
22 21 20 19 18
10 9 8 7 6 5 4 3 2 1

British Library Cataloguing in Publication Data
A full catalogue record for this book is available from the British Library.

Acknowledgements
We would like to thank the following for permission to reproduce photographs: all images by Capstone
Studio, Karon Dubke; Shutterstock: 4 Girls 1 Boy, (grid) design element throughout, telesniuk, 5,
VectorPot (gears) design element throughout.

CONTENTS

BUILDING UP AND OUT

Higher, longer, stronger, taller – we have always battled to construct the best and the biggest buildings throughout history. Skyscrapers, bridges, archways and domes are feats of human intelligence and engineering.

Learn the science behind each of these modern marvels by building them yourself. You may be starting out with boxes and tape, but one day your structures may stand as strong as brick and mortar creations.

MYSTERIES OF MASONRY

Structures built from stone, bricks or concrete blocks are called masonry. Ancient pyramids were built using masonry. You'll see many modern buildings that use it too. Do you want to be a mason? Try out this project to get a feel for how masonry works.

FACT Masons use mortar to hold bricks or stones together. Mortar is made from cement, water and sand. It bonds the bricks or blocks together. Tape works in the same way. It lets you stack your boxes much higher.

BLOCKS AND MORTAR

YOU'LL NEED

> clear tape

> 4 empty gelatin boxes

STEPS

1 Tape the open end of each box closed.

2 Put one box on its narrow side.

3 Stack another box on top.

4 Keep stacking boxes until the tower falls. How many can you stack?

5 Try the same experiment, this time taping the boxes together. How many can you stack now?

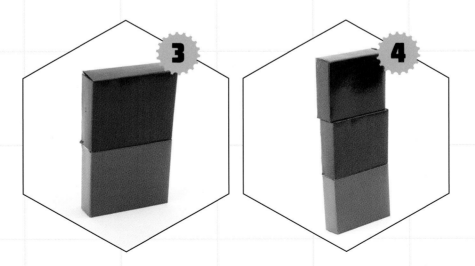

TRY THIS How many boxes can you stack? Experiment with additional gelatin boxes and use varying sizes. Does the box's size make a difference?

FOUNDATIONS AND REBAR

Heavy structures need more than blocks and mortar. They have sturdy foundations and extra support inside. See how foundations and reinforcing bars work as supports.

YOU'LL NEED

> 10-centimetre- (4-inch-) long piece of wooden 2x4

> drill with 5 mm (3/16-inch) drill bit

> 5 mm (3/16 inch) wooden dowel

> clear tape

> 10 to 12 small gelatin boxes

> awl

FACT Most bricks and concrete blocks are hollow inside. Filling these holes with mortar and steel reinforcing bars – called rebar – makes structures stronger. They can stand much taller and are more secure.

STEPS

1. Lay the 2x4 flat on a well-protected work surface. Ask an adult to use the drill to make a hole in the middle of the wood.

2. Push one end of the dowel into the hole.

3. Tape the open end of each box closed.

4. Ask an adult to use the awl to make a hole in the middle of one of the boxes. The hole should be on a narrow side of the box.

5. Make another hole on the opposite side of the box.

6. Thread the box onto the dowel using the holes.

7. Repeat steps 4–6 with the other boxes. How many can you stack?

 FACT Two things help you to stack lots of boxes on the dowel: a good foundation and good reinforcement. The 2x4 acts like a foundation under a masonry wall. A heavy structure must have a sturdy foundation to hold it up. The other thing that helps you build a tall tower is the dowel. The dowel works like the reinforcing bars that are hidden inside many masonry structures.

9

BUILD AN ARCH

Masonry blocks can be cut and shaped to make unique structural features. Many ancient and modern structures have arches made from specially shaped blocks. Try shaping your own blocks to make an impressive arch.

YOU'LL NEED

> 9 small gelatin boxes

> ruler

> marker

> sharp scissors

> clear tape

STEPS

1   Lay one box flat on your work surface.

2   Measure and make a mark 2.5 cm (1 inch) from the closed end on each side of the box.

3 Measure and make marks 1 cm (3/8 inch) from each corner along the open edge of the box.

4 Draw a line connecting the marks on each side of the box.

5 Carefully cut out these triangles.

 FACT The wedge shape of the boxes helps spread the weight of the arch evenly among each box. Many ancient builders cut their blocks so perfectly that their arches didn't need mortar! But you can use tape to hold yours together if necessary.

6 Turn the box over. Repeat steps 2–5 on the back of the box.

7 Bend the box edges in to make a wedge shape. Tape the box closed.

8 Repeat steps 1–7 to make nine wedges in total.

9 Stack the wedges to make an arch. Use blocks of wood or stacks of books to help hold the arch up as you build.

10 When you've finished building, carefully slide the blocks away.

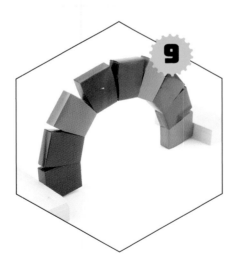

 FACT In traditional arches, the piece in the centre is called the keystone. It is placed last and locks all the blocks together.

FACT Masons build structures called falsework to hold their arches in place during construction. This falsework is removed when the arch is finished. The books or blocks of wood support the arch as you build, acting like falsework.

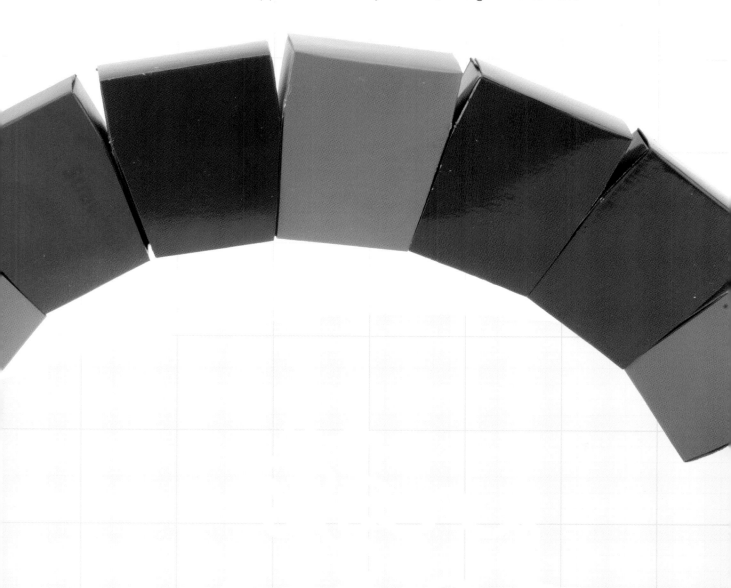

TALL TOWERS

Skyscrapers can reach over 100 storeys in height. The Burj Khalifa in Dubai, United Arab Emirates, is the world's tallest skyscraper. It's 828 metres (2,716.5 feet) tall! Do you want to play around with tall towers? Let's get to work.

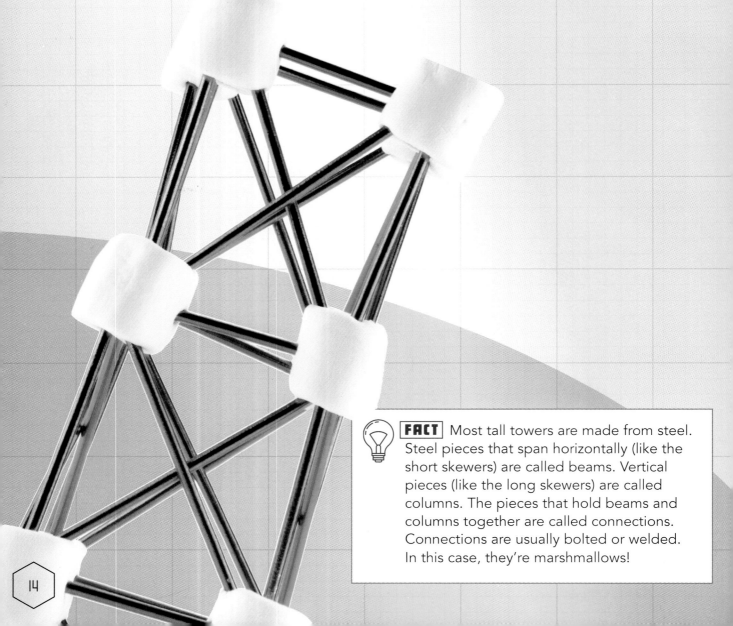

FACT Most tall towers are made from steel. Steel pieces that span horizontally (like the short skewers) are called beams. Vertical pieces (like the long skewers) are called columns. The pieces that hold beams and columns together are called connections. Connections are usually bolted or welded. In this case, they're marshmallows!

BUILD A BASIC TOWER

YOU'LL NEED

> scissors

> 7 wooden skewers

> 8 large marshmallows

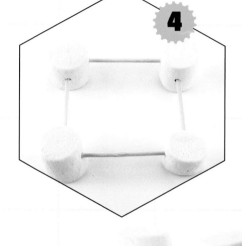

STEPS

1 Use the scissors to cut one of the skewers into three pieces of equal length.

2 Repeat step 1 with two other skewers.

3 Stand four marshmallows on their flat sides to form a square.

4 Connect the marshmallows with four short skewer pieces.

5 Repeat steps 3–4 to make another square.

6 Push the long skewers into the flat sides of the marshmallows of one square.

7 Place the other square on top of these long skewers to make a tower.

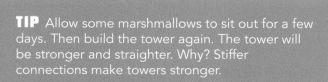

TIP Allow some marshmallows to sit out for a few days. Then build the tower again. The tower will be stronger and straighter. Why? Stiffer connections make towers stronger.

ADDING X-BRACING

Beams and columns are the basic parts of a tower. But there are other important parts too. Push down on the Basic Tower. What happens? It easily sways because it's missing some important parts. Let's see how bracing can make a tower stronger and taller.

YOU'LL NEED

> scissors
> 25 wooden skewers
> 12 large marshmallows

STEPS

1   Use the scissors, seven skewers and eight marshmallows to build a Basic Tower.

2   Connect two diagonal marshmallows with a long skewer.

3   Repeat step 2, but connect the opposite two marshmallows. You should now have an X shape.

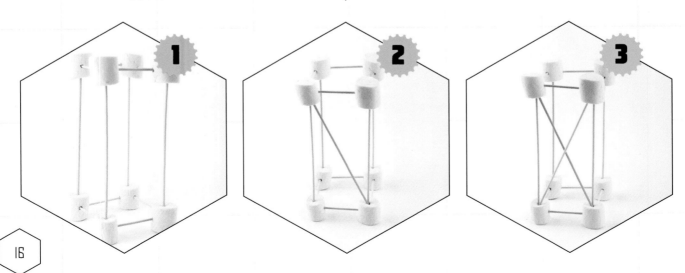

4 Continue adding X shapes around the tower.

5 Add a second level to the tower.

6 Use more skewers and add X shapes to this level.

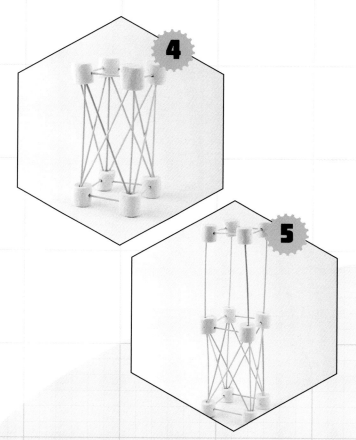

 FACT Bracing is needed to keep skyscrapers strong. You've created x-bracing in your tower. Builders also use concrete walls to brace buildings. Can you add a third level to your tower?

 FACT Braced buildings can also resist lateral forces. Lateral forces, such as wind, push on the sides of buildings. Push on the side of your tower. Does the x-bracing help?

ADDING A CANTILEVER

A cantilever is a part of a structure that is supported at one end. One example of a cantilever is a balcony. There are also cantilever bridges that are supported at each end. The cantilevered part hangs out over the water and meets a cantilever supported on the opposite shore. Can your tower support a cantilever?

YOU'LL NEED

> scissors

> 28 wooden skewers

> 14 large marshmallows

> three large binder clips

STEPS

1 Use the scissors, 27 skewers and 12 marshmallows to build a Tower With X-Bracing.

2 Stick a skewer into the top of a marshmallow. Repeat with a second skewer and marshmallow.

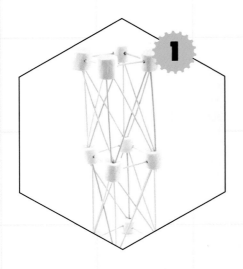

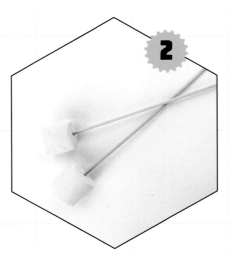

3 Cut the last skewer into thirds. Use one of the pieces to connect the two skewered marshmallows.

4 Clip the binder clips to the top level of the tower.

5 Attach your three-sided rectangle to two marshmallows at the top of the tower. The rectangle should stick out at the side of the tower.

6 Remove the binder clips one at a time. What happens?

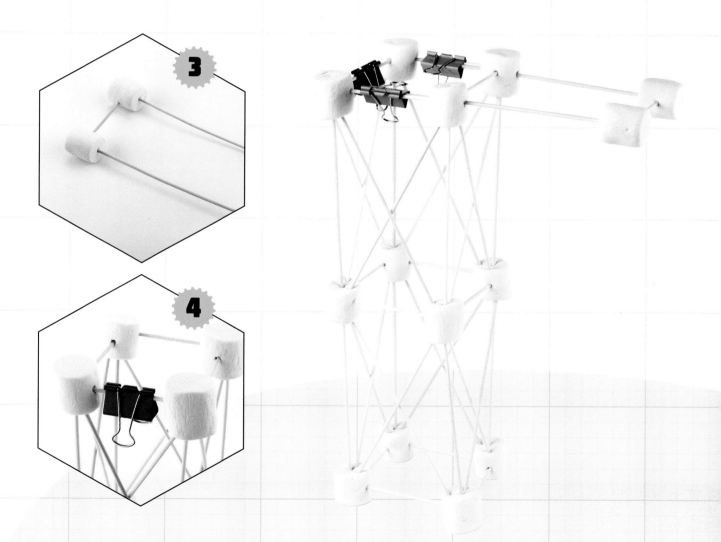

 FACT Cantilevers add a lot of weight to one side of a structure. The weight needs to be balanced. The clips create that balance. Without them, the tower becomes unstable.

TERRIFIC TRIANGLES

Think about the shape of a house. Then compare it to a block of flats or skyscraper. You might think of rectangles when you think of these structures. But look closer. Most structures contain repeating triangle shapes. Try out this project to learn why.

 FACT The triangle is the strongest structural shape. An even spread of forces keeps the triangle rigid, and it doesn't bend like a square or rectangle.

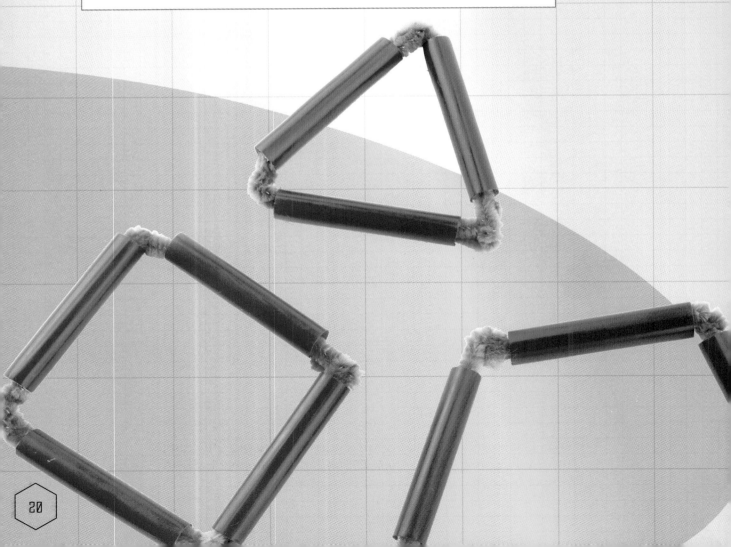

TEST OUT TRIANGLES

 **YOU'LL NEED**

> scissors
> drinking straws

> ruler
> pipe cleaners

STEPS

1   Cut the drinking straws into 5-cm- (2-inch-) long sections. Make 12 sections.

2   Cut the pipe cleaners into 10-cm- (4-inch-) long sections. Make 12 sections.

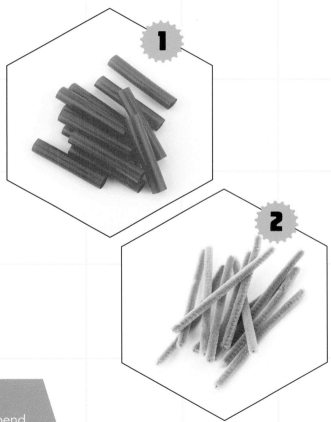

TIP If your straws are bendy, cut around the bend. Then discard that section.

3 Thread a straw onto a pipe cleaner. Repeat with all the straws and pipe cleaners.

4 Use three pieces to make a triangle shape. Twist the ends of the pipe cleaners together several times to connect the pieces.

5 Repeat step 4, but use four pieces to make a square shape.

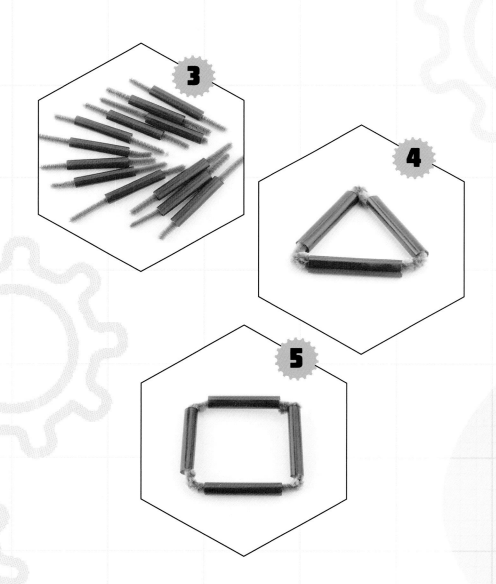

6 Repeat step 4, but use five pieces to make a pentagon.

7 Take turns standing each piece upright. Push on the top of each shape. Which is the strongest?

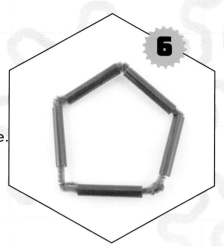

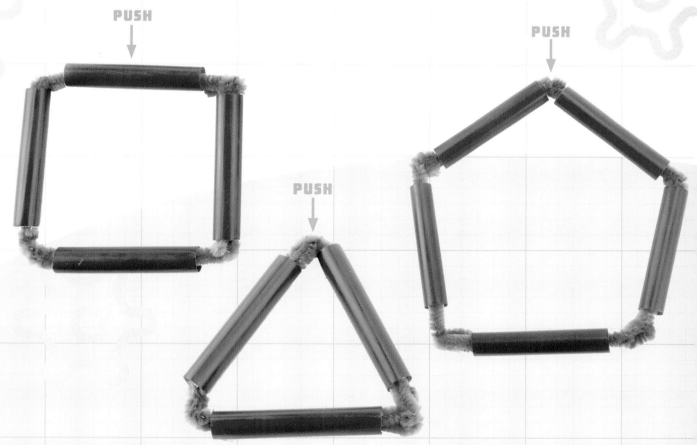

PUSH

PUSH

PUSH

FACT To strengthen squares and rectangles, you can add a diagonal piece across the middle. You now have two triangles!

TRIANGLES IN TRUSSES

We don't live in triangle-shaped buildings. But triangles play a big role in construction, even if you can't always see them. Truss bridges are triangles you can see in the real world. Build your own bridge to see how they work.

YOU'LL NEED

> scissors
> drinking straws
> ruler

> pipe cleaners
> 2 pieces of wood

STEPS

1   Cut the drinking straws into 5-cm- (2-inch-) long sections. Make 19 sections.

2   Cut the pipe cleaners into 10-cm- (4-inch-) long sections. Make 19 sections.

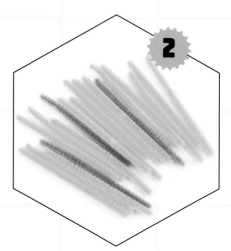

3 Thread a straw onto a pipe cleaner. Repeat with all the straws and pipe cleaners.

4 Use three pieces to make a triangle shape. Twist the ends of the pipe cleaner together several times to connect the pieces.

5 Add two pieces to one end of the triangle to make two triangles.

6 Repeat step 5 on the other end of the triangle to make three triangles. This is a truss.

7 Repeat steps 4–6 to make another truss.

8 Stand the trusses upright with the longest sides at the bottom.

9 Use three straw-and-pipe-cleaner pieces to connect the bottoms of the trusses.

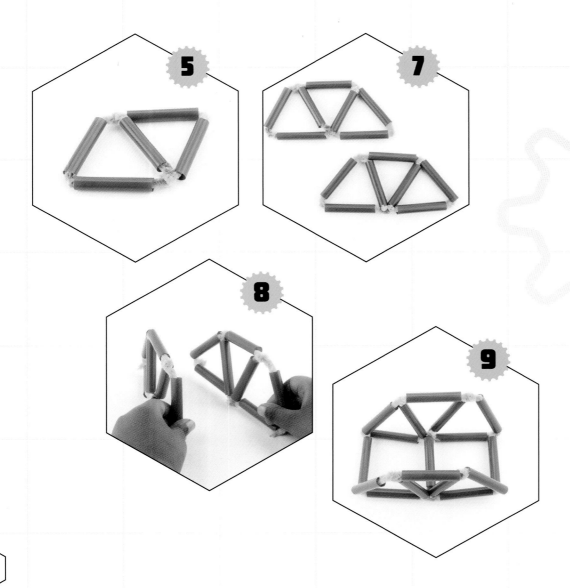

10   Use two more pieces to connect the tops.

11   Prop the ends of your truss bridge on the edges of two pieces of wood. Push on the centre of the bridge to test its strength.

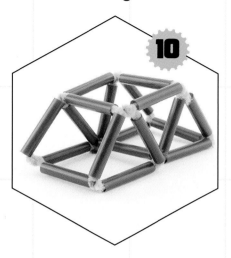

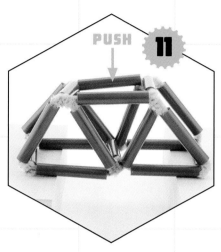

 FACT A structural shape made of repeating triangles is called a truss. The long straight pieces that make trusses are called chords. The places where they connect are called joints. Joists are structural pieces that use triangles similar to trusses. Look up in big warehouse-type buildings to see rows of joists holding up the roof.

MAKE A GEODESIC STRUCTURE

Triangles are used to make 2D structures such as joists and trusses. But their usefulness doesn't stop there. You'll find triangles in 3D structures such as domes too. The sphere-shaped Spaceship Earth at the Epcot Center in the United States is completely made up of triangles! Use triangles to make your own 3D structure.

YOU'LL NEED

> scissors

> drinking straws

> ruler

> pipe cleaners

STEPS

1 Cut the drinking straws into 5-cm- (2-inch-) long sections. Make 30 sections.

2 Cut the pipe cleaners into 10-cm- (4-inch-) long sections. Make 30 sections.

3   Thread a straw onto a pipe cleaner. Repeat with all the straws and pipe cleaners.

4   Connect five sections together to make an asterisk shape. Twist the pipe cleaner ends together several times to connect the pieces.

 FACT   Domes work well for building sports arenas or churches. They don't need support columns and are wide open inside.

5 Use five more pieces to connect the pointed ends of the asterisk. This will make a pentagon.

6 Repeat steps 4–5 to make another pentagon.

7 Connect two pieces to each point of one pentagon.

TRY THIS Domes can be full spheres or parts of spheres. Try building a full sphere out of straws and pipe cleaners.

8 Use those pieces to attach the first pentagon to the second pentagon.

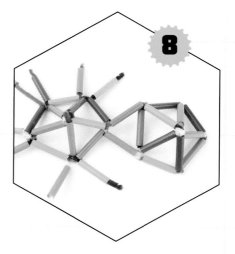

FACT You have created a geodesic structure. Buildings that are constructed using this method are called geodesic domes. They are very efficient. They enclose the most amount of space using the least amount of construction material.

BRIDGING OUT

Bridges can be used to span tiny streams or very wide channels. There are many different types, including arch, truss or girder bridges. But all of them have something in common – they need decks and supports. With a few materials, you can whip up your own basic bridge.

TRY THIS If you don't have a drill and screws, use wood glue instead. Make sure the glue is dry before adding the deck of the bridge.

BUILD A
BASIC BRIDGE

 **YOU'LL NEED**

> drill and 4-mm (5/32-inch) drill bit

> four 35-cm- (14-inch-) long pieces of 1x2 wood

> four 30-cm- (12-inch-) long pieces of 2x4 wood

> eight 3-cm (1¼-inch) plasterboard screws

> screwdriver

> ruler

> marker

> two 20-cm- (8-inch-) long pieces of 1x2 wood

> scissors

> 2 sheets of construction paper

> clear tape

> several small toy cars

STEPS

1 Ask an adult to use the drill to make a hole in the flat side of a 35 cm 1x2. The hole should be 2.5 cm (1 inch) from one end.

2 Place a 2x4 flat on your workspace. Stand the 1x2 upright against the 2x4's short side. Centre the hole along a short end of the 2x4.

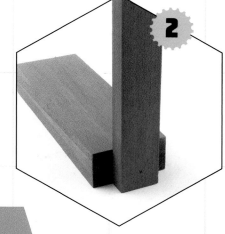

TIP Safety first! Make sure you have an adult's help with the drill. Build on a protected workspace and wear protective gear such as safety glasses and work gloves.

3   Thread a plasterboard screw through the hole. Use the screwdriver to attach the 1x2 to the 2x4.

4   Repeat steps 1–3 to make an identical piece. Stand the pieces next to each other, leaving a few centimetres in between.

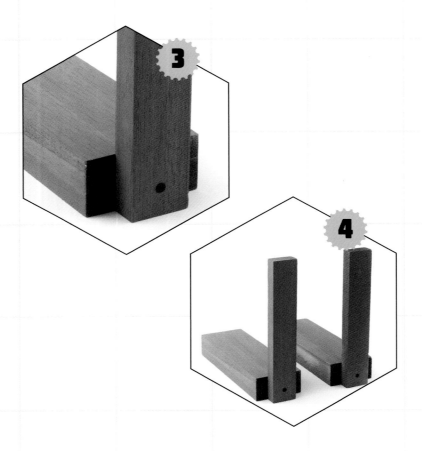

FACT The massive concrete structures at the ends of bridges are called abutments. They anchor bridges securely to the ground and support the tonnes of weight that the bridge carries.

5 Measure and mark 8 cm (3 inches) from the bottom of each 1x2. The marks should be on the same side as the 2x4s. Set aside.

6 Stand one of the 20-cm-long pieces of 1x2 on your workspace. Use the drill to make two holes on the long, flat sides. The holes should be 2.5 cm (1 inch) from each end.

7 Line up the 1x2's holes with the marks you made in step 5. Use plasterboard screws to attach the 1x2 to the 2x4s. You've just made an abutment.

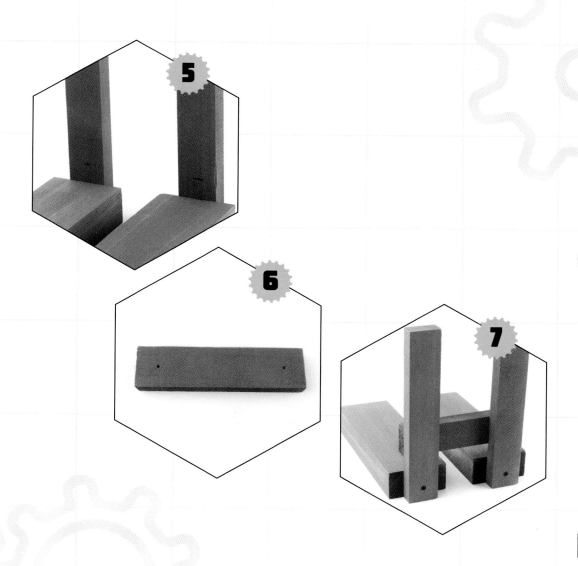

8 Repeat steps 1–7 to make another abutment.

9 Stand the abutments opposite each other. The tall 1x2s should face each other.

10 Cut the paper in half lengthways.

11 Lay three of these pieces end-to-end. Tape them together to make a deck.

12 Tape one end of the deck to an abutment's 20-cm 1x2.

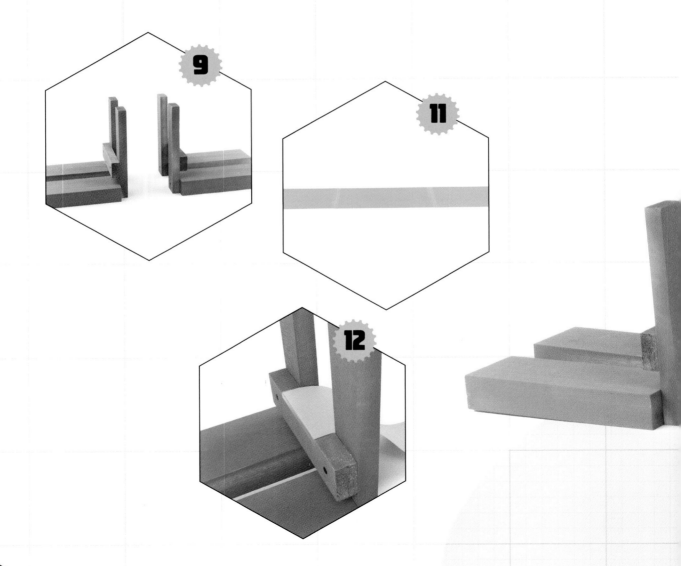

13 Tape the other end of the deck to the other abutment's 20-cm 1x2.

14 Move the abutments away from each other. Stretch the paper tight.

15 Place cars on the bridge to test its strength.

TRY THIS Some bridges have supports in the middle too. These supports are called piers. Could your bridge hold more cars if it had some piers? Slide a pile of books under the deck and test it out.

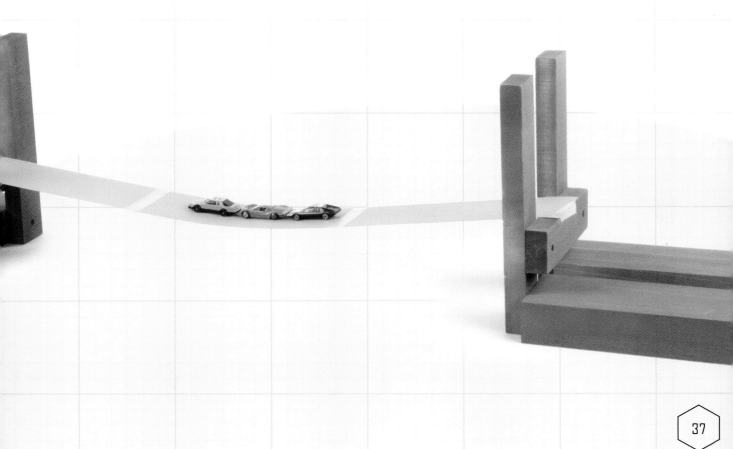

The part of the bridge that you drive or walk on is called the deck. A weak deck won't be able to carry many cars. What can you do to make it stronger?

YOU'LL NEED

> drill and 4-mm (5/32-inch) drill bit

> four 35-cm- (14-inch-) long pieces of 1x2 wood

> four 30-cm- (12-inch-) long pieces of 2x4 wood

> eight 3-cm (1 ¼-inch) plasterboard screws

> screwdriver

> two 20-cm- (8-inch-) long pieces of 1x2 wood

> 4 sheets of construction paper

> ruler

> marker pen

> scissors

> 3 drinking straws

> hot glue and hot glue gun

> clear tape

> several small toy cars

STEPS

1 Use the abutments from the Basic Bridge. Make a new deck (steps 10–11 of the Basic Bridge), but do not attach it to the abutments.

2 Place the deck flat on your workspace.

3 Measure and mark lines every 5 cm (2 inches) along the deck.

4 Cut the straws into pieces to the same width as the deck.

5 Glue a piece of straw to every line you've marked.

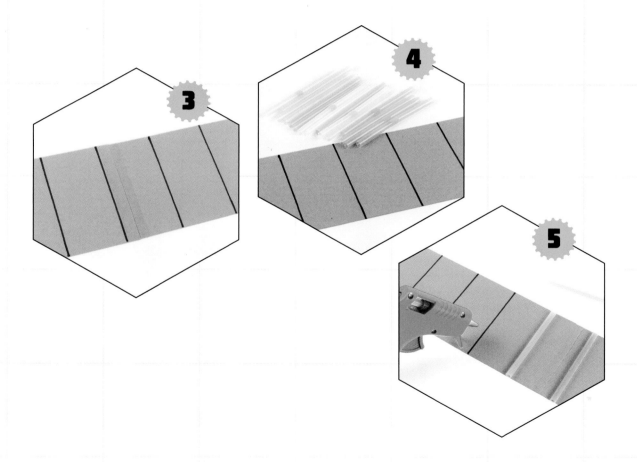

 FACT Bridge decks need support to make them strong. Adding extra layers gives that support. Beam bridges rely on heavy beams under the deck for support.

6   Cut and tape the paper you have left together
    to make a second deck.

7   Carefully glue the second deck to the top of the straws.

8   Tape the deck to the abutments.

9   Test the new deck with cars.

TRY THIS What happens if you use a more rigid material,
such as skewers or cotton buds, instead of straws? What
happens if you add another layer to your deck?

FACT Did you notice that your bridge deck slopes in the middle when you add cars? This sagging is called deflection. Bridges are designed to deflect without breaking when cars drive on them. Some bridges deflect up and down by a few metres.

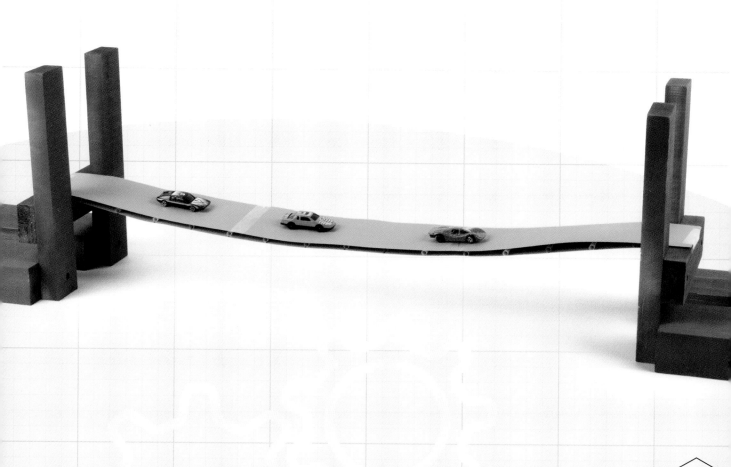

SUSPEND IT

Supporting something from the bottom makes it stronger. But it's difficult to add extra support piers under bridges that span over very deep water. Instead, these bridges are made stronger by lifting their decks from above.

YOU'LL NEED

> drill and 4-mm (5/32-inch) drill bit

> four 35-cm- (14-inch-) long pieces of 1x2 wood

> four 30-cm- (12-inch-) long pieces of 2x4 wood

> eight 3-cm (1¼-inch) plasterboard screws

> screwdriver

> two 20-cm- (8-inch-) long pieces of 1x2 wood

> 4 sheets of construction paper

> ruler

> marker pen

> scissors

> 3 drinking straws

> hot glue and hot glue gun

> clear tape

> 8 drawing pins

> large ball of string

> wooden skewer

> several small toy cars

STEPS

1 Follow the instructions for the Deck It Out bridge. Keep the deck pulled tight.

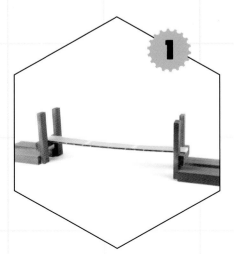

1

2 Press drawing pins into the four tall upright corners of the bridge.

3 Press pins into the end of each 2x4.

4 Cut two 1.8-m- (6-foot-) long pieces of string.

5 Tie one end of a string around one of the pins in a 2x4.

6 Pull the string tight. Wrap it several times around the pin in the upright.

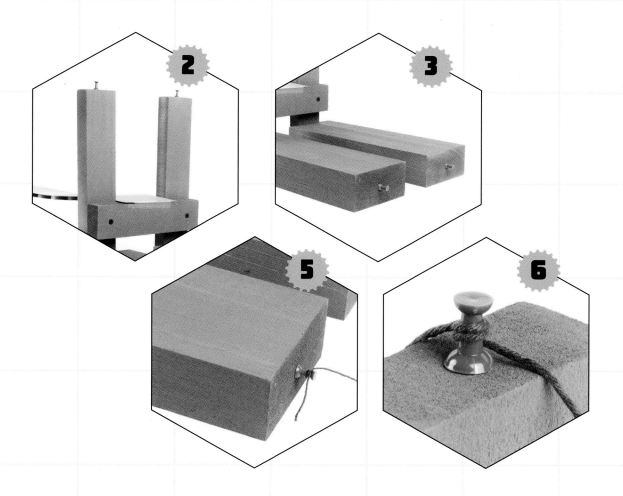

 FACT The longest pedestrian suspension bridge opened in 2017 in Switzerland. It spans 494 metres (1,621 feet) and is 85 metres (279 feet) tall at its highest point.

7   Pull the string across the bridge and wrap it around the opposite upright.

8   Tie the end to the 2x4 on that side of the bridge.

9   Repeat steps 5–8 on the other side of the bridge with the second string.

10   Cut five 1-metre- (3-foot-) long pieces of string.

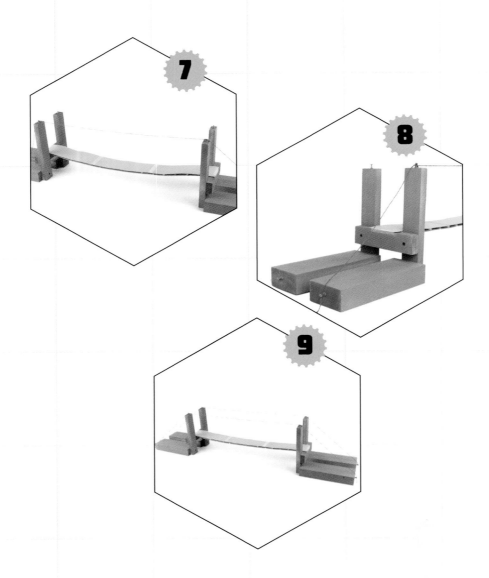

11 Tape one end of a string to the end of the skewer.

12 Thread the skewer through the straw closest to the centre of the deck.

13 Un-tape the skewer.

14 Tie each end of the string to one of the horizontal strings. Pull the string tight. Let the deck bend slightly upwards.

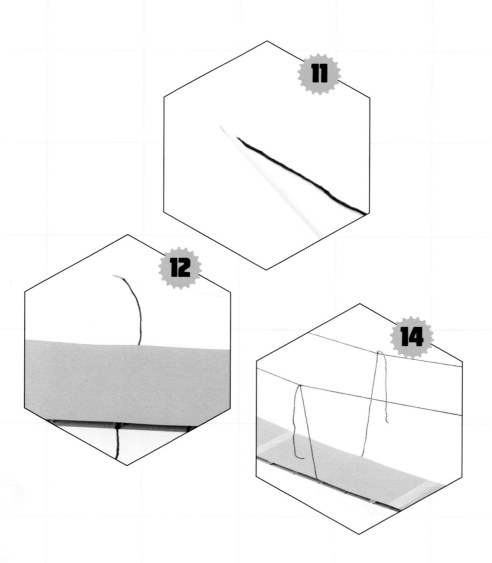

15 Cut off any extra string.

16 Repeat steps 11–15 with the remaining pieces of string. Space them evenly across the deck.

17 Test the bridge with cars.

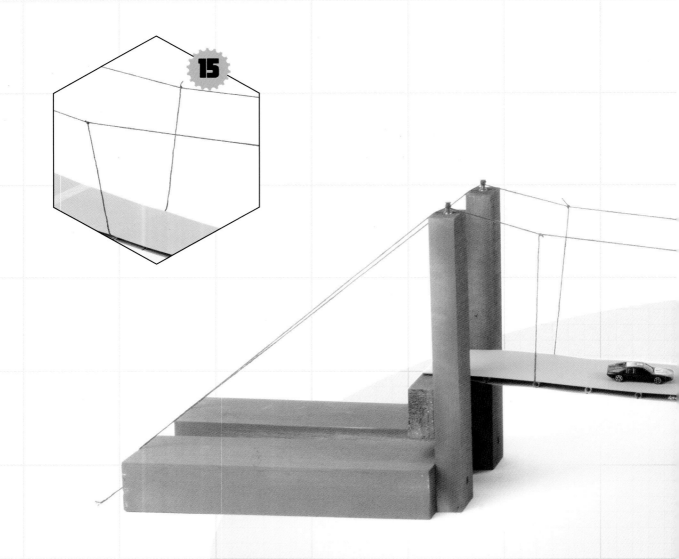

FACT You have created a suspension bridge. Suspension bridges are among the longest spanning types of bridges. The tall supports that carry a suspension bridge's weight are called towers. Strong steel cables lift the deck and carry its weight back to its supports.

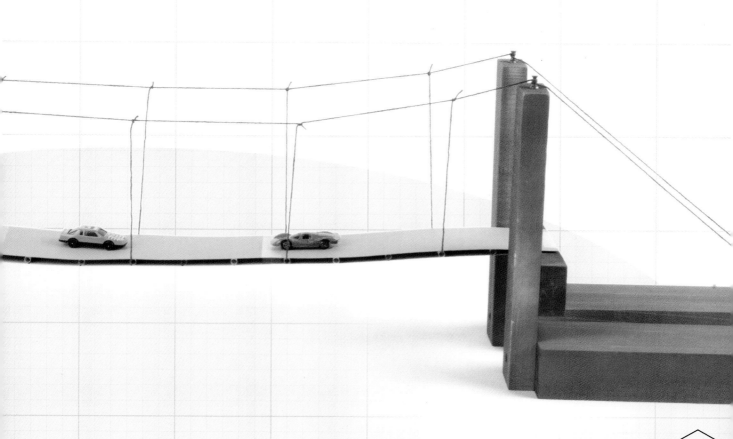

FIND OUT MORE

BOOKS

Engineering (DKfindout!), DK (DK Children, 2017)

Extraordinary Bridges (Exceptional Engineering), Sonya Newland (Raintree, 2019)

Extraordinary Skyscrapers (Exceptional Engineering), Sonya Newland (Raintree, 2019)

The World's Most Amazing Bridges (Landmark Top Tens), Michael Hurley (Raintree, 2012)

The World's Most Amazing Skyscrapers (Landmark Top Tens), Michael Hurley (Raintree, 2012)

WEBSITES

www.bbc.com/bitesize/articles/zgqpk2p
Learn more about the properties of 3D shapes.

www.dkfindout.com/uk/earth/landmarks-world/ golden-gate-bridge
Find out more about one of the most famous bridges in the world.